NATURE WATCH
ELEPHANTS

Barbara Taylor

Consultant: Dr. Adrian Lister

LORENZ BOOKS

C O N

First published in 1999 by Lorenz Books

© Anness Publishing Limited 1999

Lorenz Books is an imprint of
Anness Publishing Limited, Hermes House,
88–89 Blackfriars Road, London SE1 8HA.

Published in the USA by Lorenz Books,
Anness Publishing Inc., 27 West 20th Street,
New York, NY 10011; (800) 354–9657.

This edition distributed in Canada by
Raincoast Books, 8680 Cambie Street, Vancouver,
British Columbia, V6P 6M9.

ISBN 1 85967 639 1

A CIP catalogue record for this book is available from
the British Library

Publisher: Joanna Lorenz
Managing Editor, Children's Books: Sue Grabham
Senior Editor: Nicole Pearson
Editors: Simon Beecroft, Nicky Barber
Designer: Simon Wilder
Picture Researcher: Adrian Bentley
Illustrators: David Webb, Vanessa Card, Julian Baker
Production Controller: Ann Childers
Editorial Reader: Joy Wotton

Printed and bound in Singapore

10 9 8 7 6 5 4 3 2 1

PICTURE CREDITS
b=bottom, t=top, c= center, l= left, r= right

ABPL/ Daryl Balfour: 9al, 12bl, 23bl, 35bl; ABPL/ Nigel Dennis:
33bl; ABPL/ Paul Funston: 29cl; Clem Haagner: 37al; ABPL/Martin
Harvey: 20ar, 23cr, 34b, 36ar &bc, 37bl, 39b, 54b; ABPL/Gerald
Hinde: 9bl; ABPL/Luke Hunter: 60br;ABPL/Beverly Joubert: 6al;
ABPL/ Philip Kahl: 30cl, 34ar; ABPL/Peter Lillie: 40cl; ABPL/
Philip Richardson: 61al; ABPL/Lorna Stanton: 48ar; ABPL/Gavin
Tomson: 9br; Heather Angel: 24bl, 33cr; Ardea: 30bl; BBC Natural
History Unit/ Lockwood & Dattari: 5br; BBC Natural History Unit/
Keith Scoley: 13al; CFCL/Image Select: 4ar, 29br; CFCL/Image
Select/ Chris Fairclough: 21br; Bios/ Michel Denis Huot: 6bc, 41bl;
Bios/ Nicholas Granier: 43br; The Bodleian Library: 15al;
Bridgeman: 13ar, 25cl; Bruce Coleman/ Alain Compost: 8ar; Bruce
Coleman/ Michael Fogden: 30br; Bruce Coleman/ Paul Van Gaalen:
7bl; Bruce Coleman/M P Kahl: 23ac; Alan G Potts: 21bl; Bruce
Coleman/ Rod Williams: 54ar; ET Archive: 11cl, 53al; Mary Evans:
51cr; FLPA/ Peter Davey: 52br; FLPA/ F Hartmann: 11br; FLPA/
David Hosking: 12al, 53b; FLPA/ Terry Whittaker: 14ar; FLPA/
Martin Withers: 28b; Michael Holford: 4bl, 40ar, 55br; Kobal
Collection: 49bl; Adrian Lister: 30tl, 51br & bl; Ken Lucas: 10bl;
Natural History Museum London: 13br; Natural Science Photo
Library/ D Allen Photography: 18al, 21ar; Natural Science Photo
Library/C & T Stuart: 52ar; Natural Science Photo Library/S G
Neginhal: 55ac; Natural Science Photo Library/Pete Oxford: 19al,
52br, 56cr; Natural Science Photo Library/M W Powles: 46bl;
Natural Science Photo Library/M S Price: 59tr; Natural Science
Photo Library/P H & S L Ward: 57b; Nature Photographers/ Peter
Craig Cooper: 47cl; Nature Photographers/ Hugo Van Lawick: 5ar,
Nature Photographers/Paul Sterry: 47al; NHPA/Kevin Aitken: 52bl;
NHPA/Daryl Balfour: 19ar & bl, 20bl, 28cl, 51bl; NHPA/Anthony
Bannister: 18br, 59bl; NHPA/K Gani: 7al & ar; NHPA/Martin
Harvey: 38c, 56al &br, 57ar; NHPA/ T Kitchener/ V Hurst: 60bl;
NHPA/ Steve Robinson: 31br; NHPA/Philip Ware: 8c; Oxford
Scientific Films: 41a, 45cr; Oxford Scientific Films/ Jen & Des
Bartlett: 32ac; Oxford Scientific Films/ G I Bernard: 25al; Oxford
Scientific Films/ Martyn Colbeck: 4c, 8bl, 14bl, 22bl, 25br, 29tr, 58b,
39t, 40br, 41br, 42al, 44al, 44bl, 45cr, 45bl, 47bl, 49ar; Oxford
Scientific Films/ Cynthia Moss: 45al; Oxford Scientific Films/ Stan
Osolinski: 28ar, 32al, 33a, 46ar; Oxford Scientific Films/ Richard
Packwood: 55ar; Oxford Scientific Films/Vinay Parelkar/ Dinodia:
55al; Oxford Scientific Films/Anup Shah: 58tl; Oxford Scientific
Films/ Gavin Thurston: 14al; Oxford Scientific Films/Steve Turner:
58b; Oxford Scientific Films/Belinda Wright: 25c; Papillio: 7br;
Papillio/ John R Jones: 15ar, 55bl; Planet Earth/ K & K Ammann:
59br; Planet Earth Pictures: 49cl; Planet Earth Pictures/Thomas
Dressler: 43al; Planet Earth Pictures/Roger de la Harpe: 61br; Planet
Earth Pictures/Frank Krahmer: 21al; Planet Earth Pictures/Doug
Perrine: 53ar; Planet Earth Pictures/Jagdeep Rajput: 48br; Planet
Earth Pictures/Roger Rogoff: 22al; Planet Earth Pictures/Brendan
Ryan: 49br; Planet Earth Pictures/Jonathon Scott: 42c, 45br; Planet
Earth Pictures/Anupe Manos Shah: 42br; Ian Redmond: 10br; Ann
Ronan: 11ar; Frank Spooner Pictures/ Oliver Blaise: 22br.

T E N T S

What is an Elephant?

Elephants are the largest and heaviest creatures on land. An African male (bull) elephant weighs as much as 80 people, 6 cars, 12 large horses or 1,500 cats! Elephants are extremely strong and can pick up whole trees with their trunks. They are also highly intelligent, gentle animals. Females live together in family groups and look after one another. Like human beings, elephants are mammals. As with all mammals, they can control their body temperature and, like most mammals, they give birth to babies. After humans, elephants are the longest living mammals. Some live to be about 70 years old. Two species of elephant exist today—the African elephant and the Asian elephant. Both have a trunk, large ears and thick, gray skin. Not all elephants have tusks, however. Generally, only African elephants and male Asian elephants have tusks.

▲ **WORKING ELEPHANTS**
In India, domesticated (tamed) elephants are used by farmers to carry heavy loads. In some Asian countries they also move heavy logs by pulling them.

Tail, with a brush of thick hair at the end

Indra and the Elephant
One of the most celebrated Hindu gods, Indra, rides a mighty white elephant called Airavata. In Hinduism (the main religion of India), elephants are sacred animals. One of Indra's emblems is the ankus, a special pointed stick used to control elephants. Indra is shown holding an ankus in this painting.

▼ UNUSUAL FEATURES

The mighty elephant is a record-breaking beast. Not only is it the largest land animal, it is also the second tallest (only the giraffe is taller). It has larger ears, teeth and tusks than any other animal. The elephant is also one of the few animals to have a nose in the form of a long trunk.

FAMILY LIFE ▲

Adult male and female elephants do not live together in family groups. Instead, adult sisters and daughters live in groups led by an older female. Adult males (bulls) live on their own or in all-male groups.

The huge ear of an African elephant

Small eyes, protected by long eyelashes

Wrinkly skin with hardly any hair

Long trunk, used as a nose and an extra hand

Strong legs and flat feet for support

Gently curved tusks, used for digging, fighting and lifting

BABY ELEPHANTS ▲

An elephant baby feels safe between its mother's front legs. It spends most of the first year of its life there. Mother elephants look after their young for longer than any other animal parent except humans. All the members of the family group assist and protect the young.

African or Asian?

How do you tell an African elephant from an Asian elephant? They seem alike, but they are not identical. The most obvious difference is the size of the ears—the African elephant's are larger. In Africa, too, elephants have longer legs and a more slender body than their Asian relatives. The back of the Asian elephant is arched, while the African species has a dip in its back. Another difference is tusks —in Asia usually only males have visible tusks, whereas in Africa both male and female elephants normally have them.

▲ AFRICAN SHAPE

You can always tell an African elephant from its large ears and the dip in its back. This species of elephant usually holds its head slightly lower than its shoulders. The male African elephant stands on average 11 ft at the shoulder, while females are about 9 ft tall. The male weighs about 5 tons, which is about the same as a truck.

► CONTINENTAL EARS

Some people say that the large, triangular ears of the African elephant (*right*) are shaped like the continent of Africa, while the ears of an Asian elephant are shaped like India. In fact, ears are like finger-prints—they are different on each elephant. Scientists look closely at the pattern of veins, notches and tears on the ears to identify individual elephants.

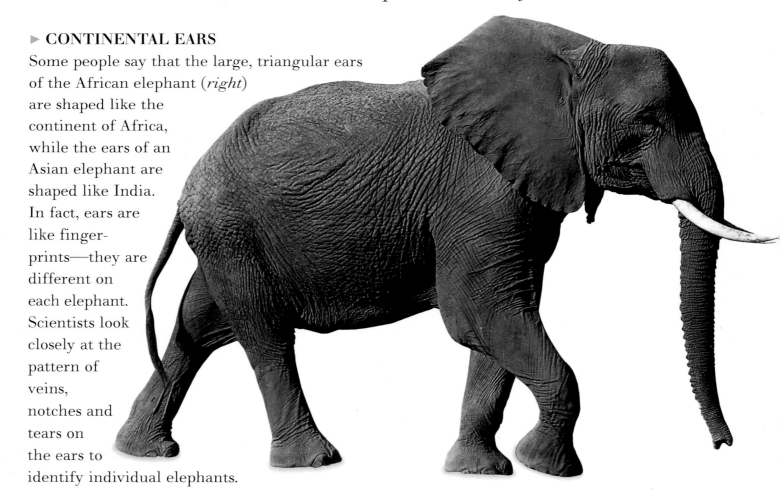

► **HEAD UP**

The Latin name of the Asian elephant, *Elephas maximus*, means huge arch. This refers to the upturned shape of its back. The Asian elephant usually holds its head above its body, so that the top of its head is the highest point of the body.

▲ **ASIAN TUSKS**

The tusks of a male Asian elephant are shorter and lighter than those of an African elephant. Female Asian elephants have very small tusks or none at all.

Did you know? The heaviest known African elephant weighed 7 tons.

▼ **SKIN SPOTS**

Elephants are usually thought of as gray. However, some Asian elephants have pink patches of skin. These patches are commonly found on the ears, trunk and face. They generally develop as the animal grows older. African elephants rarely have them.

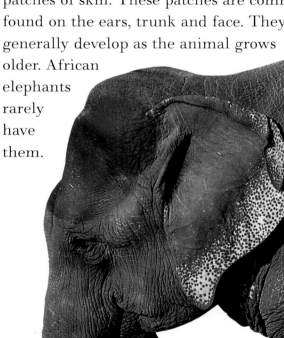

▲ **THE HAIRY ONE**

Asian elephants have more hair than their African relatives, and baby Asian elephants (*above*) are hairier still. As baby elephants grow up, most of this protective hair is worn away.

Elephant Habitats

The two main species of elephant are divided into smaller groups called subspecies. These subspecies each look a little different from one another and are named after their habitats. Africa has three subspecies—the bush elephant of the open grasslands, the forest elephant of west and central Africa, and the desert elephant of Namibia. The main subspecies in Asia is the Indian and southeast Asian elephant. Asia is also home to the Sri Lankan elephant and the Sumatran elephant, which lives on the islands of Sumatra and Borneo (parts of Indonesia).

▲ SUMATRAN ELEPHANT
These elephants wade into swamps to find juicy grasses to feast on. They are the smallest of the three Asian subspecies. Sumatran elephants are also the lightest in color, and they have fewer pink patches than the other Asian subspecies.

SRI LANKAN ELEPHANT ▶
The rare Sri Lankan elephant is the biggest and darkest of the three Asian subspecies. Many of the 2,500—2,700 elephants in Sri Lanka live in protected national parks or nature reserves.

Did you know? The desert elephant is the tallest elephant in the world, at up to 14 ft high.

◀ FOREST ELEPHANTS
The forest elephant (*Loxodonta africana cyclotis*) is the smallest African subspecies. Its size enables it to move easily through the trees. Generally, its ears are small and rounded, and its tusks are less curved than those of other African elephants.

◄ DESERT ELEPHANTS

The hot, dry deserts of Namibia in southwest Africa are home to the rare desert elephant. This subspecies is very closely related to the African bush elephant, but it has longer legs. Desert elephants have to walk long distances to find food and water. Scientists think that this is why they have longer legs than any other subspecies.

► ELEPHANT WORLD

African elephants live in a scattered band across central and southern Africa. They became extinct in north Africa around A.D. 300. Today, Asian elephants live in hilly or mountainous areas of India, Sri Lanka, southeast Asia, Malaysia, Indonesia and southern China. In the past, they roamed right across Asia.

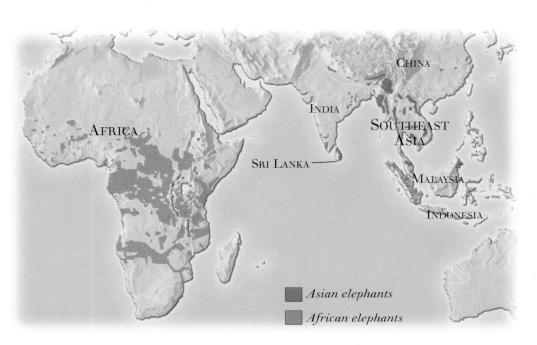

CHINA

INDIA

AFRICA

SOUTHEAST ASIA

SRI LANKA

MALAYSIA

INDONESIA

■ *Asian elephants*
■ *African elephants*

▲ BUSH ELEPHANTS

African bush elephants live on the savanna (areas of grassland with scattered trees). However, some live in forests or marshes and even on mountains.

◄ SOLIDLY BUILT

The African bush elephant, *Loxodonta africana africana*, is bulkier and heavier than any other elephant subspecies. Like all elephants, its large size is a useful weapon against lions, tigers and other predators.

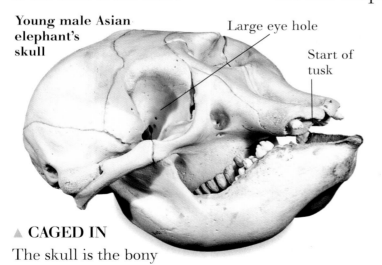

Big Bones

An elephant's legs are placed directly underneath its body, like a table's legs. This arrangement provides a firm support for its great weight. The leg bones stack one above the other to form a strong, tall pillar. As a result, an elephant can rest, and even sleep, while standing up. The pillar-like legs also help to hold up the backbone, which runs along the top of the animal and supports the ribs. The backbones of both African and Asian elephants arch upward in the middle. Their differently shaped backs are produced by bony spines that stick up from the backbone. The elephant's skeleton is not just built for strength, however. It is also flexible enough to let the elephant kneel and squat easily.

▲ BONY BACK

Long spines stick up from the backbone of the Asian elephant's skeleton. The muscles that hold up the head are joined to these spines and to the back of the skull.

Young male Asian elephant's skull

Large eye hole

Start of tusk

▲ CAGED IN

The skull is the bony box that protects the brain and holds the huge teeth and tusks. The skull above is that of a young elephant with undeveloped tusks. On an adult male the upper jaw juts out further than the lower jaw because it contains the roots for the heavy tusks.

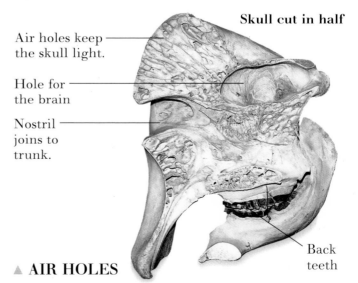

Skull cut in half

Air holes keep the skull light.

Hole for the brain

Nostril joins to trunk.

Back teeth

▲ AIR HOLES

An elephant has a large skull compared to the size of its body. However, a honeycomb of air holes inside the skull makes it lighter than it looks from the outside.

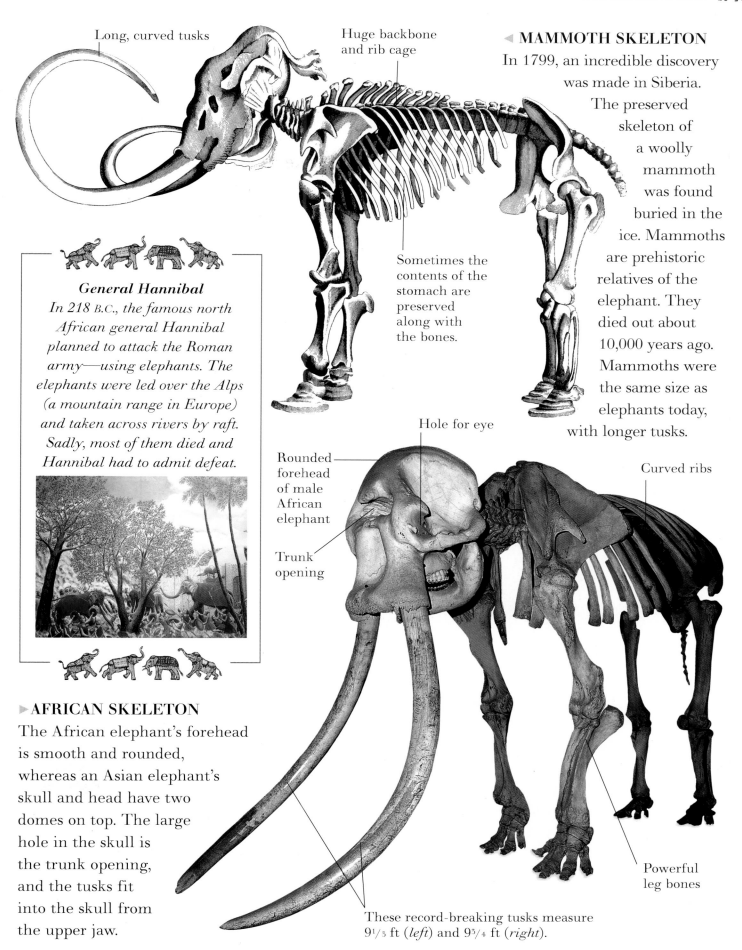

Long, curved tusks

Huge backbone and rib cage

Sometimes the contents of the stomach are preserved along with the bones.

◀ MAMMOTH SKELETON

In 1799, an incredible discovery was made in Siberia. The preserved skeleton of a woolly mammoth was found buried in the ice. Mammoths are prehistoric relatives of the elephant. They died out about 10,000 years ago. Mammoths were the same size as elephants today, with longer tusks.

General Hannibal

In 218 B.C., the famous north African general Hannibal planned to attack the Roman army—using elephants. The elephants were led over the Alps (a mountain range in Europe) and taken across rivers by raft. Sadly, most of them died and Hannibal had to admit defeat.

Hole for eye

Rounded forehead of male African elephant

Trunk opening

Curved ribs

▶ AFRICAN SKELETON

The African elephant's forehead is smooth and rounded, whereas an Asian elephant's skull and head have two domes on top. The large hole in the skull is the trunk opening, and the tusks fit into the skull from the upper jaw.

Powerful leg bones

These record-breaking tusks measure 9$\frac{1}{3}$ ft (*left*) and 9$\frac{3}{4}$ ft (*right*).

11

Tusks

An elephant's tusks are its front teeth. The part that we see is just two-thirds of the tusk's total length. The rest is hidden in the skull. Tusks are made from a very hard material called ivory. Elephants mainly use their tusks for feeding. The sharp ends are ideal for digging up edible roots and stripping bark from trees. Tusks are also used as weapons, and help to protect the trunk, like a car bumper. Elephants are born with milk tusks, which are replaced by permanent tusks when the elephant is between 6–12 months old. They grow continuously at the rate of about 7 inches a year. As the tip wears down, more tusk is pushed out from the skull.

▲ TINY TUSKS

Some female Asian elephants have small tusks called tushes. They grow so slowly that they hardly stick out of the mouth. Some male Asian elephants have no tusks.

This elephant's left-hand tusk is shorter than the right-hand one because it has been used more.

Male elephant tusks weigh up to 132 lbs, or about the weight of two children. Female tusks are lighter and weigh 20 lbs on average.

Did you know? One rare elephant was found with four tusks instead of two.

◄ TUSK SHAPES

Elephants tend to be either right-handed or left-handed, just as human beings are. Their tusks are like hands, and elephants prefer to use one of them more than the other one. As a result, the favorite one becomes more worn. Tusks also come in different shapes and sizes. Some are slim and straight, while others stick out at different angles or even cross in front.

◀ USEFUL TUSKS

African elephants dig for salt with their tusks. They loosen the soil with the sharp points, just as we use a garden rake. On occasions, elephants also dig for salt in caves underground.

▼ MAMMOTH TUSKS

The tusks of extinct mammoths could be 8–10 ft long—half as long again as the tusks of most African elephants today. Mammoth tusks tended to curve first outward and then inward, although the females' tusks were more symmetrical and smaller than the males'. Early humans hunted mammoths for food. They also built huts from the bones.

African bull (male) tusk

African cow (female) tusk

Asian bull (male) tusk

▲ FIGHTING ELEPHANTS

In ancient India, humans trained elephants to help them fight battles. The elephant's sharp tusks were deadly when used as weapons. In ancient Rome, elephants were made to battle against gladiators (trained fighters) and other animals for sport. Cruelly, the elephants were usually forced to fight against their own gentle nature.

◀ RAW MATERIALS

Tusks are made of solid ivory, which is a type of dentine. This is a hard material that forms the tusks of all tusked mammals. Nerves and blood vessels run through the tusks. The blood carries food to feed the growing tusk. Elephants feel pain and pressure in their tusks, just as we can in our teeth.

Body Parts

An elephant's skin is thick, gray and wrinkly, and surprisingly sensitive. Some insects, including flies and mosquitoes, can bite into it. Often, elephants roll around in the mud to keep flies from biting them (as well as to cool themselves down). Underneath the skin, the elephant has typical mammal body parts, only much larger. The heart, for example, is about five times bigger than a human heart and weighs up to 44 pounds—the weight of a child. Also, an elephant's huge intestines can weigh nearly a ton, including the contents. The powerful lungs are operated by strong muscles. These let the elephant breathe underwater while using its trunk as a snorkel.

▲ **THICK SKIN**
An elephant's skin is 1 in. thick on the back and in some areas of the head. But in other places, such as around the mouth, the skin is paper thin.

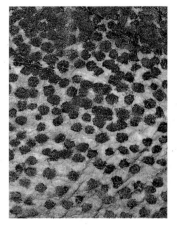

▲ **PINK SKIN**
An elephant gets its color from dots of gray pigment (coloring) in the skin. As it ages, this gray pigment may gradually fade so that the skin looks pink.

Did you know? Some very rare Asian elephants have white skin.

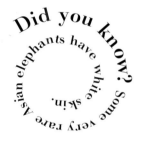

◀ **ELEPHANT HAIR**
The hairiest part of an elephant is the end of its tail. The tail hairs are many times thicker than human hair and grow into thick tufts. Apart from the end of the tail, the chin and around the eyes and ears, the elephant is not a particularly hairy animal.

▲ PINK TRUNKS

Some Asian elephants, particularly the Sri Lankan subspecies, have pink trunks. They may also have pink patches on their ears, face and belly, which are a sign of aging. This is comparable to the human hair turning gray.

Flying Elephants

According to an Indian folktale, elephants could once fly. This ability was taken away by a hermit with magical powers when a flock of elephants woke him from a deep trance. The elephants landed in a tree above him, making a lot of noise and causing a branch to fall on his head. The hermit was so furious that he cast a magical spell.

▼ INSIDE AN ELEPHANT

If you could look inside the body of an elephant, you would see its huge skeleton supporting the inner organs. The elephant cross section shown here is of a female elephant.

Ribs

Small intestine

Ovaries

Shoulder blade

Brain

Skull

Backbone

Kidney

Eye

Nostril

Uterus

Bladder

Esophagus

Trachea (windpipe)

Lungs

Stomach

Liver

Large intestine

Anus

Nerve

Heart

Nerve in trunk

Wrist bone

Blood vessel

Ankle bone

15

Elephant Senses

Elephants use their five senses to learn about their surroundings—hearing, sight, smell, touch and taste. The most important sense is smell, which they rely on more than any other. Elephants smell through their trunks, using them as directional noses. The trunk is also particularly sensitive to touch and has short hairs that help the elephant feel things. The tip of the trunk is used to investigate food, water and other objects. It can tell whether something is hot, cold, sharp or smooth. Elephants communicate with each other largely by sound. They make rumbling sounds, most of which are too low for humans to hear. Touch is also crucial for communication. When two elephants meet, each places the tip of its trunk in the other's mouth as a greeting.

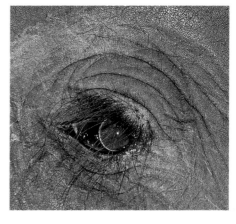

▲ **ELEPHANT EYES**
All elephants' eyes are brown with long lashes. They are small in relation to the huge head. Elephants are color blind and do not see well in direct, strong sunlight. Their eyesight is better in darker, more shadowy conditions.

Did you know? An African elephant's ear is as big as a single bed sheet and can weigh as much as a person.

◀ **SMELL**
An elephant raises its trunk like a periscope at the slightest scent of danger. It can tell who or what is coming toward it just from the smells picked up by the sensitive trunk. Its sense of smell is so powerful that an elephant can pick up the scent of a human being from more than 1 mi. away.

◀ USING EARS

An elephant strains to hear a distant noise by putting its ears forward to catch the sound. It also does this when it is curious about a certain noise. Elephants have a well-developed sense of hearing. Their enormous ears pick up the rumble of other elephants from up to about 5 mi. away. Male elephants also flap their ears to spread a special scent that lets other elephants know they are there.

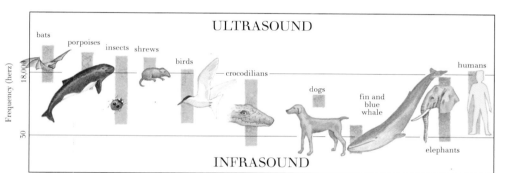

◀ HEARING RANGE

Elephants can hear low sounds called infrasound. Human beings cannot hear infrasound, although we can sometimes feel it. Some animals, such as bats and mice, can hear very high sounds called ultrasound.

▲ SENSE OF TOUCH

A young elephant is touched by its mother or another close relative every few seconds. This constant reassurance keeps it from being frightened. Elephants also touch each other when they meet. They often stand resting with their bodies touching.

▲ QUICK LEARNERS

Some young working elephants learn to stop their bells from ringing by pushing mud inside them. This allows the clever animals to steal food from farmers' fields without being heard.

Trunks

Imagine what it would be like if your nose and top lip were joined together and stretched into a long, flexible tube hanging down from your face. This is what an elephant's trunk must feel like. It can do everything your nose, lips, hand and arm can do—and more. An elephant uses its trunk to breathe, eat, drink, pick things up, throw things, feel, smell, fight and play, squirt water, mud and dust, greet and touch other elephants and make sounds. Not surprisingly, a baby elephant takes a long time to learn all the ways to use its trunk.

▲ DRINKING

An elephant cannot lower its head down to the ground to drink, so it sucks up water with its trunk. Baby elephants drink with their mouths until they learn to use their trunks to squirt water into their mouths.

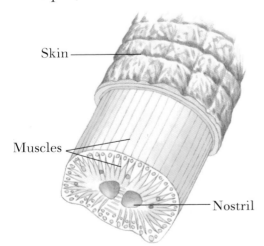

▲ A CLOSER LOOK

The two holes in the center of the trunk are nostrils, through which the elephant breathes. Thousands of muscles pull against each other in different directions to move the trunk.

▲ TRUNK POWER

An African elephant coils its trunk around a branch to lift it off the ground. Elephants can lift whole tree trunks in this way. The powerful trunk has more than 100,000 muscles, which enable an elephant to lift large, heavy objects easily.

▲ TAKING A SHOWER

An elephant does not need to stand under a shower to be sprayed with water, mud or dust. Its trunk is like a built-in shower, able to cover almost its whole body as it reaches backward over the head. Showering cools the elephant down and gets rid of insects.

▲ FLEXIBLE TRUNK

Elephants sometimes double up their trunks and rest them on their tusks. They can do this because the trunk has no bones inside it, just muscles, which makes it very flexible.

▶ TALL ORDER

African elephants use their long, stretchy trunks to pull leaves off the top branches of tall acacia trees. The highest leaves are the most juicy. The trunk is slightly telescopic, which means that, if necessary, it can be stretched out even longer than usual. The trunk can also be pushed into small holes or gaps between rocks to find hidden pools of water.

Asian elephant

African elephant

▲ TRUNK TIPS

The trunk of an African elephant has two fingers at the tip, while the Asian elephant has only one. These fingers can pick up an object as small as a leaf or a coin.

Keeping Cool

When we are hot, we lose heat through our skin, especially by sweating. An elephant cannot do this because it does not have sweat glands, so it must cool off in other ways. One way an elephant gets rid of excess body heat is by flapping its enormous ears. This increases the cooling flow of air over the body. The ears also contain blood vessels close to the skin's surface. As air blows over them, the cooled blood circulates though the entire body. Elephants cool by spraying themselves with water, mud or dust. They also love bathing in water and rolling around in mud. The mud dries on the elephant's skin, providing a barrier against the sun's heat.

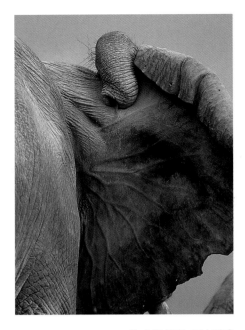

▲ **LARGE EARS**
The African bush elephant has the largest ears of all. It spends more time in open sunlight than other species, and its large ears flap, moving the air and fanning its body.

◀ **SHADY TREES**
On the African savanna, acacia trees have wide, flat tops. This makes them ideal sunshades for hot animals. Groups of elephants tend to seek out shade in the middle of the day when the sun is at its hottest.

▼ COOLING MUD

Elephants love to plaster themselves with mud, which changes their ordinary colors to vibrant reds, blacks, browns or yellows. Mud cools the skin, heals cuts, protects against insect bites and helps stop the skin from getting dry and cracked.

▲ DUST SHOWER

Dust showers are popular with elephants. An earthy coating works like mud to protect the skin from the sun's heat. It also keeps the skin in good condition.

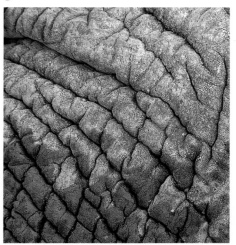

▲ BATHTIME

Zoo elephants are often given a helping hand at bathtime. In a zoo, elephants may not have enough space to spray themselves with water or dust so the keepers regularly bathe them and brush their skin to keep it in good condition.

▲ COOL WRINKLES

An elephant's wrinkled skin helps it to keep cool. Cooling water and mud are trapped in the deep folds of the skin and evaporate slowly.

SPLASHING AROUND

Elephants spray each other with water, wrestle with their trunks and flop sideways with great splashes. Sometimes they turn upside down and poke the soles of their feet out of the water. All this play strengthens the bonds between individuals and keeps groups together.

TRUNK STRAW

These two elephants are refreshing themselves at a waterhole. Elephants drink by sucking in water through their trunk. They seal off the end with the finger or fingers at the end of their trunk. Then they lift their trunk to their mouth and squirt in the water.

Focus on

Elephants love water. They drink lots of it and enjoy jumping into lakes and rivers to play and splash around. Elephants are good swimmers and can easily cross rivers or swim out to sea to reach islands with fresh food. They drink at least once a day, or more often when water is available. When water is hard to find in the wild, elephants can be very sneaky, drinking from taps, pipes or water tanks. This usually causes damaged or broken pipes. However, elephants can go without water for up to two weeks.

CHAMPION SWIMMERS

Elephants are good at swimming even though they are so big. When an elephant swims underwater, it pokes its trunk above the water and breathes through it like a snorkel.

Water Babies

KEEPING CLEAN

Frequent bathing washes the buildup of mud and dust out of the cracks in an elephant's thick skin. Disease-carrying insects and parasites that feed off the elephant's skin are also washed off in the water.

WATER BABIES

In the water, baby elephants often hold onto the tail of the elephant in front for safety. They can easily be swept away by fast flowing rivers. Baby elephants are also vulnerable to attack from crocodiles.

THIRST QUENCHER

An elephant needs to drink 18–24 gals of water a day. A full trunk of water holds about 1–3 gals. Incredibly, a very thirsty adult elephant can drink about 27 gals of water in 5 minutes.

On the Move

An elephant looks like a noisy, clumsy animal. In fact, it moves about quietly and is surprisingly agile. Forest elephants can quickly disappear into the trees like silent, gray ghosts. The secret of the elephant's silent movement is the way its foot is made. A fatty pad inside the foot cushions the impact of the foot on the ground. The sole then spreads out to take the weight of each step. Elephants usually walk slowly, at a rate of about 4 mph. They can run at more than 25 mph when angry or frightened, but only for a short distance. Elephants swim well too, and they often reach islands in lakes or off the coast. They are also good climbers, with a ridged sole that grips rough or steep ground well. However, elephants cannot jump. They would crush their legs on impact.

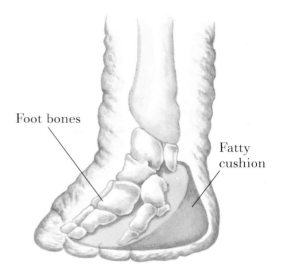

Foot bones

Fatty cushion

▲ FATTY FOOT

An elephant's enormous weight rests on the tips of its toes and on a fatty cushion that works like a giant shock absorber. This fatty shock absorber spreads out as the elephant puts its foot down and contracts as it lifts up its foot. On firm ground, the elephant leaves hardly any track marks.

Did you know? An elephant's foot measures up to 5 ft around.

◀ ELEPHANT WALK

An elephant walks and runs with shuffling steps. It cannot trot, canter or gallop. Occasionally, elephants walk backward. They sometimes find this easier than turning around, which can be a difficult maneuver for an elephant.

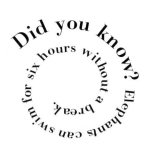

◄ GRIPPING SOLES

The skin on the sole of an elephant's foot is thick and covered in cracks and deep ridges. These help it grip rough ground effectively, rather like the treads on tires or hiking boots.

Royal Hunt
An Indian mythical story tells of King Khusraw, who was killed by his son Shirvieh. In the scene shown here, Shirvieh travels by elephant to the Royal Palace. Here he becomes caught up in a royal hunt. In India, people often rode elephants to hunt.

◄ FOOTCARE

An elephant has a thorn removed from its foot. Elephants in captivity move about less than they do in the wild. As a result, their feet are less tough and need to be looked after. Toenails are not worn away either, so they have to be trimmed.

► ON THE MARCH

A line of elephants crosses the savanna in Kenya. Elephants often march along in a row, sometimes with each elephant holding the tail of the one in front. Elephants usually walk about 16 mi. a day, but in the hot deserts of Namibia in southwest Africa journeys of up to 121 mi. a day have been recorded.

Elephant Migrations

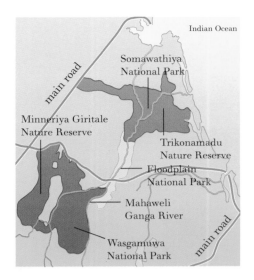

protected areas | planned extension to protected areas

▲ ANIMAL CORRIDORS
Much of the land in Sri Lanka is used for agriculture, so some elephants live in protected areas. They move between the regions along special corridors of land, in the same way that people travel between cities along highways.

Elephants do not have permanent homes. Every year they make long journeys called migrations to search for food and water. In the dry seasons, elephants gather in large groups for feeding migrations. They follow the same paths when moving from one place to another year after year. These paths are learned by one generation of elephants after another. Today, elephants have been squeezed into smaller areas as human beings take up more and more land. As a result, elephant migrations are much shorter than they used to be, although they may still cover hundreds of miles.

ELEPHANT RAIDERS ▶
Farmers on the island of Sumatra try to chase a herd of elephants away from their corn fields. Migrating elephants can do a lot of damage to crops.

◀ ELEPHANT WELLS
During times of drought, elephants may dig holes in dry stream beds. They use their trunks, tusks and feet to reach water hidden underground. Elephants need to drink 18–24 gals of water each day and have been known to travel long distances of up to 19 mi. to reach a tiny patch of rainfall. Elephant wells can be lifesavers for other wildlife that come to drink the water after the elephants have gone.

LONG JOURNEYS ▶
African elephants on the savanna grasslands may wander over an area of more than 1,860 square mi. The extent of their migrations depends on the weather and other conditions. Asian elephants living in forests migrate over smaller areas of about 60–180 square mi.

◀ **WATCHING FROM ABOVE**
Migrating elephants can be followed by airplane in open country. Little or no rain falls during the dry season and the elephants tend to group together in places where water is available. The thirsty animals usually stay around a river valley or a swamp that still has water in it. In rainy seasons, elephants spread out over a wider area.

◀ **ELEPHANT BARRIERS**
Elephants will try anything to find a way through farmers' fences. They can use their tusks to break electric fence wires and even drop large rocks or logs on top of fences.

KEEPING TRACK ▶
Scientists in Africa fit a radio-collar to an elephant. This device tracks the animal's movements without disturbing its natural behavior.

Feeding

Elephants are herbivores (plant-eaters). They eat more than 100 different kinds of plants and enjoy almost every part—from the leaves, twigs, bark and roots to the flowers, fruit, seeds and thorns. Most plants are not very nutritious however, so an elephant has to eat huge amounts to survive. It spends about 16 hours a day choosing, picking and eating its food. Millions of microscopic organisms live inside an elephant's gut, which help to digest food. Even with the help of these organisms, half the food eaten by an elephant leaves the body undigested.

◢ STRIPPING BARK

An elephant munches on tree bark, which provides it with essential minerals and fiber. The elephant pushes its tusks under the bark to pull it off of the tree trunk. Then it peels off a strip of bark by pulling with its trunk.

◄ EATING THORNS

Elephants do not mind swallowing a mouthful of thorns—as long as some tasty leaves are attached to it! Leaves and thorns make up an important part of an elephant's diet as they stay green in the dry season long after the grasses have dried up. This is because trees and bushes have long roots to reach water deep underground.

▼ GRASSY DIET

Marshes are packed full of juicy grasses. About 30–60 percent of an elephant's diet is grass. On dry land, an elephant may even beat grass against its leg to remove the soil before feeding.

Did you know? Elephants can become drunk by eating overripe fruit.

▶ **BABY FOOD**

Baby elephants often feed on the dung of adult elephants. They do this to pick up microscopic organisms to live inside their gut and help them digest food. Baby elephants learn what is good to eat by watching their mother and other relatives. They are also curious and like to try new types of food.

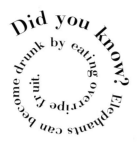

◀ **DUNG FOOD**

Elephant dung provides a feast for dung beetles and thousands of other insects. They lay their eggs in the dung, and the young feed on it when they hatch. Certain seeds only sprout in dung after having first passed through an elephant.

FOOD IN CAPTIVITY ▶

People make meals for captive elephants from grasses and molasses (a type of sugar). Zoo elephants eat food such as hay, bread, nuts, fruit, leaves, bark and vegetables. They need a huge pile of food every day—in the wild they eat 220–440 lbs of plants every day.

29

Teeth

▲ **EARLY TOOTH**
This fossilized mammoth's tooth is 8 in. long. The pattern of ridges on the tooth resembles that of an Asian elephant rather than an African elephant.

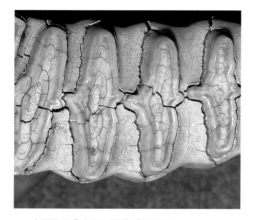

▲ **AFRICAN TOOTH**
The ridges on an African elephant's tooth are lozenge (diamond) shaped. The scientific name of this elephant, *Loxodonta*, means lozenge teeth.

▲ **ASIAN ELEPHANT TOOTH**
The ridges on the surface of an elephant's tooth act like scissor blades. They cut up food as the elephant chews.

An elephant's front teeth are its tusks. They stick out from the mouth. An elephant also has molar teeth inside its mouth. The tusks are only in the top jaw, but the molars are in both the top and the bottom jaw. Two molars sit on each side of the mouth, each one weighing more than a brick. Sharp ridges along the top of the molars grind up tough plants. Tusks grow continuously, but molars gradually wear down and drop out. New teeth develop behind the old ones and slowly move forward along the jaw to take their place. An elephant goes through six sets of molar teeth in a lifetime—that is 24 molar teeth altogether. Each new tooth is bigger than the one before. After the sixth replacement set, the elephant is no longer able to chew its food properly.

▲ **CHEWING UP FOOD**
An elephant uses just four huge teeth inside its mouth at any one time. It has two in the top jaw and two in the bottom jaw. Its lower jaws move back and forth to chew. This pulls and pushes the food against the grinding ridges of the molar teeth.

▶ CONVEYOR-BELT TEETH

An elephant's teeth come through at the back of the mouth, move forward and wear out at the front. Once a set of molars has lost its effectiveness, replacement sets of molars are in reserve, ready to push in from behind. The first teeth are replaced at 1–2 years old, the second at 3–4 years, the third at 8–10 years, the fourth around 20–25 years and the fifth at 35–40. The sixth set of molars must last the elephant for the rest of its life.

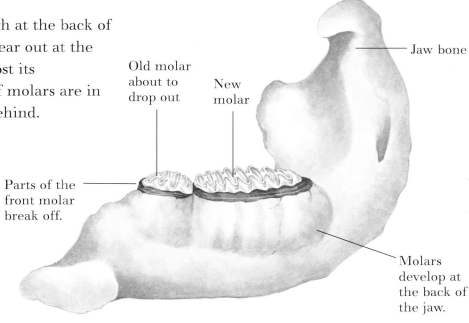

Jaw bone

Old molar about to drop out

New molar

Parts of the front molar break off.

Molars develop at the back of the jaw.

◀ OPEN WIDE

The positions of the molar teeth inside the mouth of an African elephant can be seen by peering down its throat. The mouth is relatively small and delicate and the tongue is fleshy.

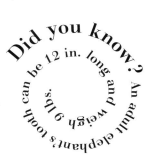

Did you know? An adult elephant's tooth can be 12 in. long and weigh 9 lbs.

▲ LONG IN THE TOOTH

Scientists work out the age of an elephant by looking at its teeth. When the animal loses its last tooth, it cannot chew its food properly and soon dies of malnutrition.

Focus on

An elephant's day follows a regular pattern of feeding, sleeping and traveling to new feeding areas. Meeting, greeting and communicating with other elephants is an important part of every day and interrupts other activities from time to time. Feeding takes up most of the time—about 16 hours a day. They also need to drink a lot of water and bathe to cool off. Elephants sleep twice a day, once for a few hours at noon and again in the early hours of the morning. They usually sleep standing up, but sometimes they lie on their sides.

LIQUID REFRESHMENT

Elephants usually drink only once or twice a day. As they stroll along in their endless search for food, they have to make sure they do not wander too far from the nearest waterhole. Sometimes their migration routes follow rivers.

MEALTIME

When an elephant feeds, it may close its eyes or gaze off into the distance. Seeing its food is less important to the animal than touching and smelling it. The elephant uses its trunk to feel for food.

STICKING TOGETHER

Adult elephants help babies cross rivers. Young elephants have to keep up with the rest of the herd as it wanders over large areas searching for food and water. However, adult elephants cooperate with each other to protect and guide the young of the herd. When danger is sensed, the group forms a tight circle around the calves. The matriarch (female leader) faces the direction of the threat.

Daily Life

AT PLAY
Elephant calves play together for part of every day. They chase, push and climb over other babies and wrestle with their trunks. These playful calves are testing their strength and learning to live in the group.

TIME FOR A NAP
Usually, elephants sleep standing up, supported by their firm, rigid legs. They may rest their trunks on the ground while they snooze. At other times, elephants sleep lying on their sides. When they do this, they have been known to make pillows of grass for themselves. Sleeping elephants have also been heard snoring.

NIGHT REFRESHMENT
A group of elephants has a cool night-time drink at a water hole in Namibia, southwest Africa. Elephants use their keen senses of smell, touch and hearing to find their way in the dark. When feeding at night, they also make rumbling noises to let each other know where they are. Family members like to eat at the same time.

Living Together

An elephant family group is made up of related females and their offspring. Each family is led by an older, dominant female known as the matriarch. She makes all the decisions for the group. Her experience, learned over many years, is very important in keeping the family healthy and safe. Female elephants never leave the matriarchal unit unless it becomes too big. Then smaller groups break away and are led by the eldest daughters. Bulls (male elephants) leave their family group when they are between 10 and 16 years old. When they are adults, only the strongest males mate with the females. Bulls spend most of their lives in small, all-male groups (comprising two or three animals) or wander on their own. Each family group has close links with up to five other families in the same area. These linked family units, together with groups of adult bulls, make up a herd.

▲ LITTLE LEARNERS
Young elephant calves copy the adults of the family to learn where to find water and food. If they are in trouble, a big sister, a cousin or an aunt is always around to help.

▼ THE MATRIARCH
Usually, the oldest and largest adult female becomes the matriarch (female leader). The rest of the group relies on her. She controls when they eat, drink and rest. She also protects them from danger and controls family members who misbehave.

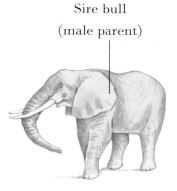

Sire bull
(male parent)

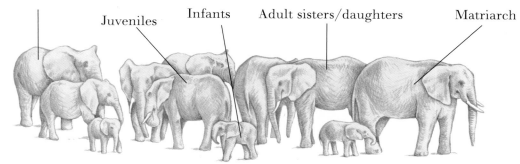

Young bulls

Juveniles

Infants

Adult sisters/daughters

Matriarch

▲ AFRICAN FAMILY

A family of African elephants usually consists of a matriarch, her adult daughters and sisters, their calves and a number of young males and females. Bulls may sometimes join the family for mating, but they do not stay with it for long. They soon leave to resume their solitary lives.

◄ ASIAN FAMILIES

Elephants in Asia live in smaller groups than African elephants. Asian families have between four and eight members, although as many as 10–20 individuals may stay in touch.

◄ ALONE

Young bulls have a lot to learn once they leave the safety of their families. Often, they follow older males (patriarchs) around, and sometimes they have mock fights. However, males do not form strong social bonds with each other as the females in family groups do. As a result, some bulls lead entirely solitary lives.

Communication

Everyone knows the loud trumpeting sound that elephants make. They trumpet when they are excited, surprised, angry or lost. This sound is just one way in which elephants can communicate with one another. They also touch, smell, give off chemical signals and perform visual displays, such as the position of the ears and the trunk. Their sense of smell can even tell them about another elephant's health. Elephants also make a wide range of low, rumbling sounds that carry for many miles through forests and grasslands. Different rumbles might mean "Where are you?" or "Let's go," or "I want to play." Females can signal when they are ready to mate, and family members can warn each other of danger.

▲ **ELEPHANT GREETING**
When elephants meet, they touch each other with their trunks, smell each other and rumble greeting sounds. Frightened elephants also touch others for reassurance.

▶ **BODY LANGUAGE**
Elephants send visual signals by moving their ears and trunk. Spreading the ears wide makes the elephant look bigger. This sends a message to a potential attacker to stay away. The elephant also stands up extra tall to increase the threat. It raises its tusks and shakes its head, making its ears crack like whips against its sides.

Did you know? Humans can only hear about one third of the sounds an elephant makes.

◄ SPECIAL SOUNDS

An elephant makes its familiar high-pitched trumpeting call. Elephants also make a variety of crying, bellowing, screaming, snorting and rumbling sounds. Asian elephants make sounds that African elephants do not, and many of their rumbles last for longer. There are over 20 different kinds of rumble, with females making many more rumbling sounds than males. Females sometimes make rumbling calls when they are together, but male elephants do not do this.

▲ ALARM SIGNALS

This nervous baby elephant watches the crocodiles lying on the river bank. It raises its ears, either in alarm or as a threat to the crocodiles. If a baby calls out in distress, its relatives rush to its side, with rumbles of reassurance and comforting touches with their trunks.

▲ TOUCH AND SMELL

An elephant's skin is very sensitive, and touch is an important way of communicating feelings in elephant society. Smells also pass on useful messages, such as when a female or male is ready to mate.

Babar

One of the most famous elephants in children's literature is Babar the elephant king. He was created by French writer Jean de Brunhoff. Babar rules over the Land of the Elephants with the help of his wife Queen Celeste and his old friend General Cornelius. He fights wars with the rhinos, escapes from the circus and has many other exciting adventures.

JUST PRACTICING

Young bulls sometimes have pretend fights. They push and charge at each other, clash their tusks and wrestle with their heads.

Focus on

Male and female elephants live separately most of the time. When young male elephants become adults (at between 10 and 16 years), they are chased away from their family herd. Young bulls then form loose bonds with other males and only visit family groups occasionally. They learn from older males how to fight other males, search for females and mate with them. Bulls compete with each other to become the dominant (top) male elephant in their area. Only dominant bulls mate with the females. This helps produce healthy, strong babies. Bulls stay near a family herd only when a female is ready to mate, but they will also help to defend the herd.

IN MUSTH

About once every year, adult bulls go through a period of unpredictable, aggressive behavior called musth. A bull in musth oozes a sticky fluid from the side of his face.

FINDING A MATE

Female elephants prefer to mate with the biggest bulls. Males keep growing until they are between 35 and 45 years old. Females stop growing at about 25 years.

Bull Elephants

ESTABLISHING CONTROL

Adult bull elephants wrestle with each other to decide who is dominant and most likely to mate with the females. The bulls push and wrestle with their heads, trunks and tusks, sometimes even lifting their opponent's front legs off the ground. Eventually, the weaker bull gives up and is chased away.

BACHELOR HERDS

Young bulls sometimes form small groups for a while, called bachelor herds. These groupings are only temporary, however, and bulls lead a lonely life compared with females.

▲ **FIGHTING BULLS**

In ancient India, people liked to watch bull elephants fighting. They used bulls in musth because the bulls were then in a fighting mood.

Courtship

Male and female animals meet each other and select a mate by a process called courtship. For adult bulls this can happen at any time, but a cow can only mate on a few days every 16 weeks. During this time, she gives off special scents and makes sounds to attract bulls. When the bulls get close, she may begin walking with her head held high while looking back over her shoulder. A bull then follows her around, stroking her with his trunk. At the same time, he tries to chase away other bulls. Large bulls in musth (a period of heightened sexual desire) are best at doing this, as they put all their energy into mating. Eventually, the cow may allow the bull to mate with her. The pair stays together for a few hours or a few days.

▲ **MEETING UP**

An African bull elephant meets up with the cows in a group when they are ready to mate. A cow is first ready to mate from about 8–18 years of age, depending on the environment she lives in and the amount of food available.

▼ **THE THRILL OF THE CHASE**

During African elephant courtship, bulls may chase after cows. Depending on her mood, the cow may stop and allow the bull to mate with her, or just keep running. Cows can run faster than the large, heavy bulls.

▲ TESTING THE WATER

When a female is in heat (ready to mate), her urine has a different smell. This musth bull is smelling the female's urine to find out if it has the mating smell. He will curl the tip of his trunk into his mouth to blow the scent over two small openings in the roof of his mouth. These openings detect the scent of a female in heat.

▲ COURTSHIP CONTACT

Elephants often touch each other with their trunks during courtship. African bulls may lay their trunk and tusks along the female's back. In Asia, a bull and a cow elephant face each other and entwine their trunks together.

▲ MATING

During the act of mating, the bull elephant stands on his back legs and supports his huge weight on the cow's back. Mating can last for up to three minutes and may take place every two or three hours for a few days.

41

Birth and Babies

Female elephants are pregnant for nearly two years. They give birth to their first calf when they are between 10 and 20 years old. After that, they can produce a calf every 4–6 years until the age of about 50, when the birth rate slows down. A female elephant can have between 5 and 12 babies in a lifetime. Female elephants in the same group often have babies at about the same time and look after their young together. In areas where dry seasons make food hard to find, most births take place during rainy seasons. A young calf is highly vulnerable. Its mother feeds it milk for up to six years and protects it from enemies such as lions and tigers, yet about a third of all calves do not survive. Some drown or are crushed by falling trees.

▲ BIRTH TIME

When a baby elephant is born, it emerges from the cow in a protective covering called a birth sac. The other females sniff the newcomer and softly touch it all over, while rumbling with excitement.

A baby elephant practices using its trunk.

▲ TRUNK TRICKS

Baby elephants are curious and inquisitive. They want to touch and feel everything with their trunks. At first, they cannot control their long, wobbly nose. They trip over it or suck on it—just as human babies suck their thumbs. It takes months of practice to learn how to use the trunk.

▶ NOURISHING MILK

A calf suckles milk from its mother's breasts with its mouth. The milk is thin and watery, but very nourishing. Babies put on weight at a rate of 22–44 lbs per month.

◄ LEARNING FAST

A young elephant has to master giving itself a dust bath. It must also learn to pick up and carry things with its trunk, drink, feed, and have a mudbath. If a young elephant cannot reach water, the mother sucks up water in her trunk and squirts it down her baby's throat.

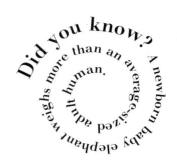

Did you know? A newborn baby elephant weighs more than an average-sized adult human.

GUIDING TRUNK ►

At first, a baby elephant sticks close to its mother night and day. It is always within reach of a comforting touch from her strong, guiding trunk. The mother encourages her baby, helps it keep up with other members of the herd and often pulls it back if it starts to stray. Baby elephants will die quickly if they are left on their own.

▲ PROPER FOOD

After a few months, calves begin to eat plants. At first, a calf may put its trunk into its mother's mouth to test which plants are edible.

▲ HELPFUL RELATIVES

The survival of both mothers and calves depends greatly on the support of the family group. Each member takes part in bringing up the babies so that young elephants learn to care for calves, too. This support also gives the mother a break.

Focus on

Giving birth can be quite a dangerous time for elephants because the pregnant female is particularly vulnerable to attack. To protect her, other females may form a large circle around her. More experienced relatives, known as midwives, usually help with the birth. The whole birth process takes only about an hour. Within two hours of birth, the calf usually begins to take its first shaky steps. The mother often takes it to meet the rest of the family group. The other elephants greet the arrival of the new calf with great excitement.

1 Most female elephants squat to give birth. Occasionally, they give birth lying down. Cows are often restless during the time it takes for the calf to emerge. The other females may trumpet and scream to keep away predators.

2 The female elephant has to push as hard as possible to force the calf out of her body. Finally, the calf begins to emerge from between its mother's back legs. A female relative usually stands nearby to act as a midwife and help the struggling mother through this difficult time.

Giving Birth

3 Sometimes a baby elephant is born feet first. It emerges still partly inside the protective sac in which it has spent the last 22 months in its mother's belly. Amazingly, the delivery of the calf is fairly quick and lasts only about half a minute. After the birth, the midwife encourages the mother to push out the afterbirth (the material that helps support, feed and protect the baby while it is in the womb).

4 The mother and the midwife together remove the sticky birth sac from around the newborn baby. The mother then eats the afterbirth, which is full of vitamins and nutritious hormones. They help her produce milk as quickly as possible in order to feed her newborn calf. She usually recovers her strength after a short time.

5 A calf can usually stand on its feet within about an hour of its birth. Nevertheless, its mother helps support it with her feet and trunk for a while longer. Once the newborn calf gets to its feet, it is guided to its mother's nipple for its first drink of milk. Her nipples are situated on her belly, between her front legs.

Growing Up

A baby elephant is brought up by its family in a fun-loving, easygoing and caring environment—in spite of the dangers. At first, a calf spends a lot of time with its mother. Then, as it grows older and stronger, it is allowed more freedom to explore and it begins to make friends with other calves. Calves spend a lot of time playing together. They can do this because they feed on their mother's milk and do not have to find food all day. Gradually the calf learns all the skills it needs to survive on its own.

▲ **BROTHERS AND SISTERS**

An older calf may cling to its mother for reassurance even after it has learned to feed itself. A female elephant may have calves every four to six years. Usually, just when the first calf can feed itself, another one arrives.

Did you know? Female elephants become adult in nine or ten years, but males mature a few years later.

◄ **MOTHER'S MILK**

A calf drinks its mother's milk until it is between four and six years old. By then, the mother usually needs her milk for the next baby. Even so, calves as old as eight have been known to push a younger brother or sister out of the way to steal a drink.

◄ **PLAYTIME**

A growing elephant learns a lot simply by playing. Male elephants push and shove each other to test their strength. Females play games with lots of chasing, such as tag. Both males and females like to play in mud, dust or water.

▲ **PROTECTING THE YOUNG**

All the adults in a family are protective of the young. They shade calves from the sun and stand guard over them while they sleep. Small calves are vulnerable to attack from many predators, including poisonous snakes.

Ganesh

In the Hindu religion of India, Ganesh is the elephant-headed god of wisdom and the remover of obstacles. Ganesh's father, the god Siva, is said to have cut off Ganesh's head. His mother, the goddess Parvati, was so angry that she forced Siva to give her son a new head. This new head turned out to be that of an elephant. Hindus seek good luck from Ganesh before the start of important business.

◄ **LOTS OF MOTHERS**

Aunties, also called allomothers, take a special interest in the upbringing of calves. They wake the calf up when it is time to travel, help it if it gets stuck in mud and protect it from danger.

47

Life and Death

While elephant calves often fall prey to crocodiles and big cats, it is hard to imagine how an animal as big and powerful as an adult elephant can be harmed. Adult elephants have no serious predators other than people, who kill them for their ivory tusks or destroy their habitats. Yet elephants can also be killed by diseases, accidents, droughts or floods, just like any other animal. When an elephant dies, members of its family try to pick it up. They may throw dust or leaves on the body and stand over it for hours. Elephants also seem to remember where family members have died.

▲ **DROUGHT**

Elephants gather by rivers and swamps during a drought. Food and water is in short supply at this time. For heavy water users like elephants, lack of water can be fatal. Drought is the most likely cause of death in African elephants, after being hunted by humans.

Did you know?
Elephants can recognize the body of a dead relative.

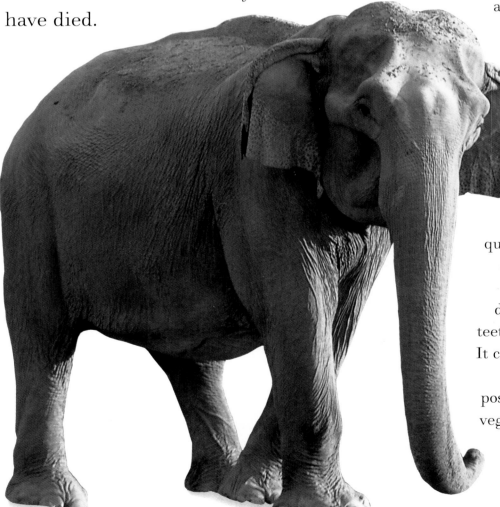

◀ **OLD AGE**

Older elephants move less quickly than others. The group slows down to wait for them. When an elephant has worn down its sixth and final set of teeth, feeding becomes difficult. It cannot grind up and digest its food properly. Whenever possible, it feeds on soft, watery vegetation at swamps and lakes. Eventually, feeding becomes impossible altogether, and the elephant collapses and dies from malnutrition.

► FASCINATING BONES

Elephants appear to be fascinated by the bones of dead elephants. They feel, sniff and scatter them around. Sometimes, the animals pull out the tusks from the skull and smash them. They may even carry bones around in their mouths for a time or bury them. Chewing bones may also be a way of obtaining the mineral calcium, which is contained in bones and teeth.

An elephant gently touches the body of a dying family member to try to rouse it.

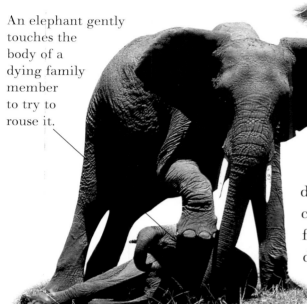

◄ RESPECTING THE DEAD

A dying elephant is comforted by another family member, who touches it gently with its trunk. If a family member dies, the group often lingers for days, apparently showing respect for the dead. They comfort any bereaved calves. If a young calf dies, the mother may carry it around on her tusks for a while. When elephants come across the body of a dead elephant, they smell or touch it all over.

▲ ELEPHANT GRAVEYARDS

In stories and films such as *Tarzan of the Apes*, elephants slip away to secret communal places to die. The belief in elephant graveyards arose when people found large collections of bones in one place. Actually, these places were probably the last watering holes of drought-stricken elephants.

▲ KILLING AND CULLING

In the past, people used to kill elephants for sport. Today, this is usually banned or strictly controlled, although poachers still shoot elephants illegally. Elephants may also be killed when there are too many of them in an area and there is nowhere else for them to go. This is called culling. The idea is to leave space for a smaller number of elephants to survive.

Ancestors

The two species of elephant today are the surviving members of a once huge group of animals. The early members looked nothing like elephants, however. *Moeritherium*, which lived 50-60 million years ago, was a dog-sized animal with no trunk. This creature evolved into a larger animal called *Palaeomastodon*, with tusks, long lips and jaws for feeding. The first true elephant ancestor, *Stegodon*, evolved about 12 million years ago. It gave rise to the African and Asian elephant, as well as the now extinct mammoth.

▲ **EARLIEST ANCESTOR**

Moeritherium was a small animal that lived in and around lakes and swamps about 50-60 million years ago. It had nostrils instead of a trunk, which were high on its face for breathing whilst submerged. Its eyes were also set quite high, similar to those of a hippopotamus, to allow it to see easily while in the water. *Moeritherium* had sturdy legs, like an elephant, and small tusks.

GOMPHOTHERIUM ▶

This distant elephant ancestor was up to 10 ft tall. Its skull was longer than that of a modern elephant, and it had tusks in both the top and bottom jaws. The lower jaw was longer, so the short lower tusks reached out as far as the upper ones.

◀ *STEGODON GANESA*

Stegodon ganesa lived in India and is named after the Hindu elephant-headed god Ganesh. It probably lived in forests and ate bamboo shoots and leaves. The long tusks of this animal were parallel along most of their length and grew very close together. The family to which this elephant belonged was similar to, but distinct from, true elephants. It died out about one million years ago.

50

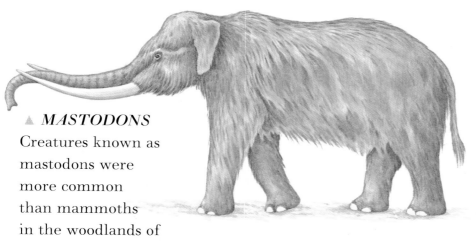

▲ MASTODONS

Creatures known as
mastodons were
more common
than mammoths
in the woodlands of
North America. They lived more than 10,000 years ago and
were about the same size as Asian elephants, with long black-
brown hair. Some mastodons had two small tusks in the lower
jaw as well as the big, curved tusks in the top jaw.

▶ WOOLLY MAMMOTHS

These elephant relatives lived
in cold areas. They had long,
woolly coats to protect them
from freezing temperatures.
Mammoths
lived at the
same time as
early humans and died
out about 10,000 years ago.

The Cyclops

*In Greek legend, Cyclops
were fierce giants with only
one eye. The legend may
have been based on the
fossilized skull of a
mastodon found in Greece.
The huge nose opening
could have been mistaken for
a large, central eye socket.*

▼ PRESERVED SKULL

Mammoth skeletons, including skulls, have
been found in Asia. From their preserved
flesh, we can determine that mammoths had
small ears. They would have
helped stop the animal
from losing
valuable body
heat in very
cold areas.

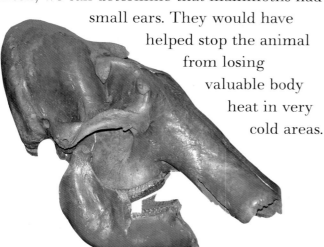

▲ CAVE PAINTING

Stone Age people painted pictures of mammoths
on cave walls, many of which can still be seen
today. These early humans may have dug pits to
trap mammoths or driven them over cliffs.

Relatives and Namesakes

Elephants do not look much like any other mammals alive today, yet they have some unlikely-looking relatives. In fact their closest living relatives are manatees and dugongs, which live in rivers, swamps and seas. Another animal that is closely related to elephants is about the size of a squirrel. It is called a hyrax and lives among rocks or in trees. The tiny elephant shrews of Africa may also be distant relatives. Evidence for these relationships comes from studying fossils and from comparing the bones and internal organs of living animals. Scientists also compare the DNA of different animals. DNA is a chemical that is passed on from parent to offspring. It is very similar in closely related animal groups.

▲ ELEPHANT SHREWS

This tiny mammal is named after its trunk-like snout, which it uses to find insects to eat. The DNA of elephant shrews is similar to the DNA of elephants, which suggests that they are related.

▼ HYRAXES

The hyrax has several features in common with the elephant. For example, both have ridges on their teeth and similar foot bones.

◄ DUGONGS

These elephant relations live in the western Pacific and the Indian oceans. They are the only vegetarian sea mammals. Dugongs, like elephants, are social animals and live in groups. Male dugongs also have tusk-like front teeth.

Mermaids

In seafaring legend, mermaids and mermen were strange creatures with human bodies and fish tails. They caused shipwrecks, floods and other disasters. These legends may have begun when sailors first saw manatees or dugongs. These animals suckle their young in a similar way to humans, yet the fish-like tail of a manatee or a dugong looks like that of a mermaid or merman.

▲ MANATEES

The manatee, like its relative the dugong, is a plump, slow-moving, vegetarian. Manatees and dugongs are sometimes called sea cows. This is because they graze on sea plants just as cows graze on land plants. Sea cows swim as whales do, using their flippers and tail.

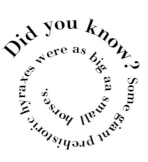

Did you know? Some giant prehistoric hyraxes were as big aa small horses.

▶ ELEPHANT SEAL

Despite its name, the elephant seal is not related to the elephant. It gets its name from the long, trunk-like nose of the male. Female elephant seals do not have the huge, swollen noses. During the breeding season, male elephant seals roar at their rivals, and the nose works like a loudspeaker.

Life with People

For thousands of years, people have hunted elephants for their meat or ivory. They have also captured and trained elephants to carry out tasks such as fighting in battles, carrying loads and pulling heavy logs out of forests. Some elephants are also used in cultural and religious ceremonies, while others are trained to entertain people in circuses or zoos. Many parts of dead elephants are used in traditional Chinese medicines, including the eyeballs to treat eye diseases. Today, both scientists and tourists ride on the backs of elephants in order to study or watch other animals in the wild.

▲ **ZOO ELEPHANTS**
Zoos and wildlife parks can help elephant conservation through education, research, fund raising and careful breeding. The best zoos keep small herds in large grassy paddocks to imitate the elephants' own habitats.

◄ **ON SAFARI**
In Africa, some elephants are used to take tourists on wildlife trips called safaris. The elephants can easily walk through tall grass and over rough ground where vehicles cannot go. Also, dangerous animals such as tigers and rhinoceros respect the elephant's great size and strength.

◀ CEREMONIAL ELEPHANTS

These elephants are taking part in an elephant march in South India. This is a competition to decide which of the elephant riders have the most colorful and striking umbrellas. Another Indian festival features a parade of colorfully painted elephants draped with rich cloth.

▲ TOURIST ELEPHANTS

In the past, hunters with guns shot animals from the backs of elephants. Now the shooting is done with cameras by tourists on organized elephant safaris. In Africa, fewer elephants are used for this purpose than in Asia. This is because there is no tradition in Africa of training elephants for work and ceremonial purposes.

▲ CIRCUS ELEPHANTS

Elephants have appeared in circuses since Roman times. They can be trained to perform tricks, although circuses with animals are becoming increasingly rare today.

◀ ELEPHANTS IN WAR

Ancient Indian war elephants wore armor and were used to trample on the enemy. Soldiers rode on top of the elephants in a wooden castle known as a howdah.

Focus on a

Elephants were first tamed and made to work about 5,000 years ago. In Asia today, between 14,000 and 17,000 elephants (about a third of all elephants in Asia) are put into service. In the past, they were caught in the wild and tamed before being trained. Now, most working elephants are born in captivity. Training usually begins when the elephant is about ten years old. It finishes when the animal is about 25. The process can be cruel. The elephant may be tied to a tree without food or water for days in order to break its spirit.

SADDLE UP
This elephant is being trained in Thailand, southeast Asia. It has to learn to accept a rider on its back and must wear a wooden saddle with chains for dragging logs. Trained elephants may be used to help train others.

BATHTIME
Working elephants enjoy a daily bath. It helps the keeper and the elephant establish a friendship and learn to trust each other.

ELEPHANT-BACK
Elephants are still the best form of transport in many areas. They move through hilly forests and cross rivers more easily than trucks. Elephants do not burn costly fuel or pollute the air, and they have longer working lives than many machines.

Working Life

HEAVY LOAD

Some elephants today are used to carry loads in hilly areas where it is difficult for vehicles to move easily. An adult elephant can carry a load weighing up to 1,100 lbs on its back. Elephants are not well suited to heavy carrying, however. They have weak shoulders and high ridged backbones.

MAHOUTS

A working elephant usually has one trainer or handler for its whole working life. In India, trainers are called mahouts. In Myanmar (Burma), they are called oozies. The trainers control their elephants with up to 60 words of command. In addition, they touch the elephant with their feet or hands. A spiked stick called an ankus is used during training to help reinforce commands.

LOGGING

In southeast Asia, elephants are used to transport heavy logs. Many people are concerned that the logging industry is destroying the forest homes of many animals including elephants themselves.

Facing Extinction

Today, elephants are in great danger. Wildlife experts warn that the species faces extinction and must be protected if it is to survive in the future. Asian elephants are most at risk, with only between 36,000 and 44,000 individuals left in the wild. In Asia, the main cause of the decline is humans taking the elephants' land. Activities such as building houses, mining, growing crops and constructing dams take up a lot of space. In Africa, the biggest threat is the ivory trade. African elephants have bigger tusks than Asian elephants and are therefore more sought after. Although the ivory trade was banned in 1989, it will take a long time for elephant numbers to recover.

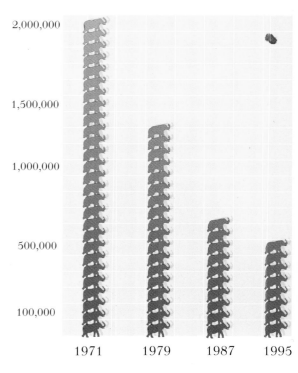

ON THE DECLINE ▲
Between 1971 and 1989, the number of elephants in Africa more than halved, from 2 million to 609,000. Up to 300 were killed each day. Over 90% of these elephants were killed illegally by poachers.

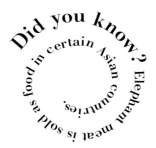

Did you know? Elephant meat is sold as food in certain Asian countries.

◄ IVORY BONFIRE
In 1989, the Kenyan government burned $3.6 million worth of ivory on this huge bonfire. They did this in order to support the worldwide ban on the trade in ivory. However, poachers will go on killing elephants illegally as long as people are prepared to pay huge sums of money for the tusks.

◄ WHITE GOLD

People have carved ivory into many objects for tens of thousands of years. Carvings in mammoth ivory have been found that date back 27,000 years. In ancient Egypt both hippopotamus and elephant ivory was carved. It is easy to carve but also hard enough to last, with a smooth, white surface. Ivory has been so prized that people have hunted elephants to almost extinction.

▲ POACHING

When poachers kill elephants, they only want the tusks. They leave the rest of the elephant to rot. Before the ban on ivory trading, an African poacher could earn hundreds of dollars for just one pair of tusks. It would take the poacher a year to earn this much money in an ordinary job.

▼ ELEPHANTS OR PEOPLE?

These elephants are invading a farmer's home and fields in Kenya, east Africa. The human population of Kenya is expected to double by the year 2020, putting enormous pressure on the land. Finding enough land for both people and elephants will be a problem. Elephants will not be able to roam freely, as they have been able to do in the past, but will be confined to special areas.

▲ TOO MANY ELEPHANTS

African elephant feet are sometimes sold to raise money for conservation. These animals were legally killed in a National Park where elephant numbers had grown too high.

Conservation

▲ CAPTIVE BREEDING
A zoo elephant has its foot cleaned with a hoof knife. Zoos play a role in conserving animals. However, elephants are not often bred in zoos because bulls are difficult to handle and can be dangerous.

Elephants need to be conserved if the species is to survive. Many African and Asian countries have set aside areas of land called national parks or nature reserves. Here, elephants are protected from the threat of poachers. This is not a perfect solution, however. Elephants in reserves are so well protected that their numbers steadily increase. Eventually, they eat themselves out of food. The rangers are then forced to kill some elephants to let others live. Other conservation efforts include keeping elephants on game ranches and banning trade in ivory. Alternatives to the ivory trade, such as plastics, resins and the nuts of a South American palm tree, are less damaging to wildlife.

▲ WALRUS WORRIES
When the trade in elephant ivory was banned in 1989, poachers turned their attention to walrus ivory instead. During 1989, poachers in speedboats shot at least 12,000 Alaskan walruses, whose tusks can grow almost 3 ft long.

▲ POACHING PATROLS
Guards in a national park in southern Africa hold wire traps left by poachers. Protecting elephants from poachers is dangerous work. As well as removing traps left for elephants, guards may become involved in gun battles as poachers try to kill elephants.

◄ ELEPHANT TRAVELS

Sometimes, elephants are moved to areas where they have a better chance of survival. Moving elephants is not an easy thing to do, however. Getting these enormous, heavy animals into a truck or an airplane can be a tricky business. Sometimes a whole family is moved, which helps these sensitive animals get over the trauma. They then settle into their new home more easily.

◄ SUPPORT GROUPS

Conservation groups such as Elefriends in the United Kingdom raise money to help conservation work in the wild. They also persuade people not to buy and trade ivory.

▲ ORPHAN BABIES

With a great deal of patience, care and understanding, orphaned baby elephants can be raised in national parks in Africa and returned to the wild. Raising a baby elephant is just as hard work as raising a baby human.

► TOURIST TRAPS

Tourists pay to watch elephants in national parks. This money is used to help run the parks and take care of the elephants. It is also used to improve the lives of people living nearby. Many of these people have given up their land to save the elephants.

GLOSSARY

afterbirth
All the material which protects and sustains a baby in its mother's womb. This is pushed out of her body after the birth.

allomother
A female elephant that helps a mother elephant to give birth and to care for her young.

ankus
A wooden pole ending in a metal point, usually with another hook set about 2 in. back from the tip. It is used to prod working elephants in order to reinforce the commands given by their trainers.

bull elephant
An adult male elephant.

bush elephant
The subspecies *Loxodonta africana africana*, which lives in the savannah grasslands of Africa.

calf
A baby elephant.

conservation
Protecting living things and helping them to survive in the future.

cow elephant
An adult female elephant.

culling
Legally killing animals when there are too many to survive in one area. The idea is that culling some animals will leave more food and space for the remaining animals and help them to survive.

dentine
A hard substance, also called ivory, which makes up the bulk of the teeth of animals with backbones. It is made of similar materials to bone.

desert elephant
A possible subspecies of the African elephant, which lives in the deserts of Namibia.

DNA (deoxyribonucleic acid)
The genetic material inside the cells of most living organisms. It controls the characteristics that are passed on from parents to their offspring.

dominant animal
A "top" animal that leads others of its own species and refuses to defer to any other member of its group.

drought
A long period of dry weather when no rain falls.

domestication
The process of bringing an animal under human control.

Elephas maximus
The Latin name for an Asian elephant.

evolution
The gradual development of new types of living things from existing species over very long periods of time.

forest elephant
The subspecies of African elephant, *Loxodonta africana cyclotis*, which is smaller than the bush elephant and lives in forests rather than grasslands.

fossils
The preserved remains of living organisms, found in rocks.

herbivore
An animal that eats plants.

herd
A large group of elephants, made up of several family units, together with groups of adult bulls. A large herd can consist of as many as 500-1,000 individual elephants.

Hinduism
One of the world's oldest religions, which began in India more than 5,000 years ago. Hindus worship several gods, and most Hindus believe that people have a soul that does not die with them but moves from body to body.

infrasound
Very low sounds which are too low for people to hear.

intestine
Part of an animal's gut where food is broken down and absorbed into the body.

ivory
The dentine of teeth, usually that of tusks, such as those in elephants, walruses or narwhals.

Loxodonta africana cyclotis
The Latin name for an African elephant.

Mahout
The Indian word for an elephant keeper, who tames and trains a working elephant.

mammal
An animal with fur or hair and a backbone, which can control its own body temperature. Female mammals feed their young on milk made in mammary glands (breasts) on their bodies.

mammoth
A large, wooly coated relative of the elephant that lived in cold places and died out about 10,000 years ago.

mastodon
Prehistoric elephants that lived in the woodlands of North America, but are now extinct.

matriarch
The experienced female elephant that leads a family unit in the wild.

migration
A regular journey some animals make from one habitat to another because of changes in the weather or their food supply, or in order to breed.

Moeritherium
A very early semi-aquatic elephant ancestor with only tiny traces of tusks and a trunk.

molar
A broad, ridged tooth in the back of a mammal's jaw, used for grinding up food.

muscle
An animal tissue made up of bundles of cells that can contract (shorten) to produce movement.

musth
A period of aggressive, dangerous behavior in bull elephants when they pick fights with other bulls and search for females that are ready to mate.

parasite
A living thing that lives on or in the body of another species, called its host, usually causing the host some harm.

pigment
Coloring matter.

poaching
Capturing and/or killing animals illegally and selling them for commercial gain.

predator
A living thing that catches and kills other living things for food.

prehistoric
The period before people wrote down any historical records.

savannah
Hot grassland with scattered trees that has wet and dry seasons.

snorkle
A breathing tube a swimmer holds in their mouth so they can breathe while swimming just below the surface of the water.

species
A group of animals that share similar characteristics and can breed together to produce fertile young.

Sri Lanka
Country off the coast of India.

Stegodon ganesa
The most advanced of the prehistoric elephants in the mastodon group. *Stegodon ganesa* is believed to be a direct ancestor of the elephant.

subspecies
A species is sometimes divided into even smaller groups called subspecies, which are sufficiently distinct to have their own group.

tush
The short tusk of an Asian or African elephant.

tusk
Long pointed tooth sticking out of an animal's mouth when it is closed.

INDEX